The Official Koosh Book

by
John Cassidy
and
Scott Stillinger
(Koosh Ball inventor)
Klutz Press • Palo Alto, CA

Grateful Acknowledgements:

Janie Benson
Mark Button
The Klutzniks, despite themselves

Design, production by Betty Lowman

Illustrations by Ed Taber

Koosh® is a registered trademark of Oddzon Products, Campbell, California, and is meant to refer to their Koosh® brand rubber ball. Use of the trademark in this publication is under an arrangement with Oddzon Products. Activities described in the following text are meant to be performed with the Koosh® brand ball. In the interests of readability, the trademark Koosh® is occasionally used in reference to the Koosh® brand rubber ball.

Published by Klutz® Press, Palo Alto, California

Manufactured in the United States of America

ISBN 0-932592-23-6

9 8 7 6 5 4

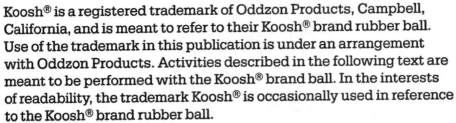

Additional Copies:
Additional copies of this book may be ordered directly from the publisher. Please see last page for details, but check with your local bookseller first.

Introduction

Let's start by answering a couple of immediate questions:

1. What IS this thing?

And…

2. What do I do with it?

And while we're at it,

3. How do they make these things, anyway?

Abner Doubleday undoubtedly had the same response when he presented the first baseball to a puzzled pre-baseball public.

Fortunately, a lot of thought has been given to these questions. We'll take them one at a time:

Q What IS this thing? Actually, we have several answers to this one. Here are some of our favorites:

A. **1.** A rubber ball with manners. Won't bounce around, roll under the furniture or skitter off unexpectedly. It's like a tennis ball after therapy. The Koosh ball can bring a quality game of catch within the reach of most anybody. (In fact it makes every game that needs a ball a little friendlier.)

2. Fruit mold from the planet Blubber. **3.** A cross between a porcupine and a bowl of jello. **4.** An eraser with a botched permanent. **5.** A fur ball from a rubber cat. **6.** Gumby's toupee. **7.** A ball bearing from an alternate universe.

The second question, "What do you DO with this thing?" is best answered by referring to pages 4–68.

The answer to the last question, "How do they make these things?" gets a little technical since The Koosh Machine represents a quantum jump in both the theory and technology of rubberized micro-mops.

In outline, old tennis shoes and eraser dust are carefully fed through an industrial food processor equipped with a special attachment...

Actually, the Koosh ball was invented when Scott Stillinger and his children began looking around for a rubber ball with training wheels. The three of them had become frustrated with the traditional tools of catch. Bean bags, tennis balls, foam rubber balls... everything either bounced too much, offered no good grip, or hurt when it bopped you.

After a while, the qualities of the Ideal Catching Implement became pretty clear to Scott. It would have to be bounceless, ouchless, tactile, and highly grabbable. Slowly, the idea of something with rubber filaments began to form in Scott's mind; something like a ball of rubber spaghetti.

There followed months of engineering-type problems and general head scratching. (Scott has a degree in mechanical engineering, but no previous experience in rubber spaghetti.) The problems were eventually solved though, and in October 1987, the first Koosh ball squirmed off the production line.

Lacroosh

This is lacrosse without the pads. You'll need one Koosh ball, and for everybody who's playing, a strainer with a handle on it. Get it out of the kitchen drawer with all the funny utensils in it.

1 Practice catching and throwing the Koosh ball with your strainer. Incidentally, the little strainers are easy to throw from, but hard to catch with. It's the opposite for the big ones, although they're preferable if you can find one. The best way

4

to "throw" out of a strainer is a shot-put kind of heave. Slinging the Koosh ball generally puts it on your foot.

2 Find an open space to play in and separate everybody into 2 teams. The more people you have, the larger space you'll need. Start from one end of the field and toss the ball to a teammate. If you have the ball, you can't move, you have to get rid of it before the other team counts to 5, slowly.

3 If you drop the ball, or hang on to it too long, the other team gets it. Also, if the other team knocks it down mid-flight, or intercepts it, they get it. First team to catch the Koosh ball over the back line on their side of the field is the winner.

Kooshdown!

Koosh Races

Flathead Racing

Place the Koosh ball directly on top of your head and race somebody else similarly handicapped. Any drops have to be picked up and replaced while standing still.

Impossihopping

Bend one foot behind you and place the Koosh ball on its sole. Then try to hop to the finish line. Drops have to be stopped for and replaced before going on. Good luck.

Wiggle Racing

Drop the Koosh ball down the back of your shirt and without touching it, maneuver it all the way through your clothing till it emerges at the bottom of your pants, shorts, dress or whatever. Pick it up off the ground and start a regular footrace. At the end, you have to do it again before you're finished.

Team Racing

This requires at least 4 people. Each team has to separate itself by some member of the other team. As each team runs to the finish line, the Koosh ball has to be thrown continuously back and forth between members. No holding on to the ball.

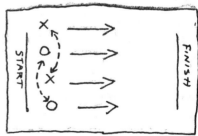

7

Dodge Koosh

A variation on an old classic, only with the sting taken out of it.

1 You'll need at least 4 players, maybe even as many as 8 or 9. In addition, you'll need a wall you can safely pelt with Koosh balls.

2 One of the players is the thrower. The others are all dodgers.

3 Find a wall with sidewalk, dirt, or pavement at the base of it. The dodgers have to stand up against the wall and stay within their square.

4 The thrower backs off 10 giant steps and takes aim. The object is to bop one of the dodgers. They can twist, jump, bend or wrinkle themselves in any way, so long as they don't get out of their squares.

5 A successful bopping counts as a point against the dodger. Misses count as points for him. Any dodger who collects 3 points switches with the thrower.

9

Bombardment

A classic gym game that works well with the Koosh ball outdoors. You need two teams of at least 3 or 4 each and a playing area about the size of a basketball court. Two front lawns are good, half a tennis court is perfect.

1 Draw a line down the middle of the field, pick your teams and separate onto the two halves. You can play with one, two, or three Koosh balls.

10

2 The idea is to hit one of your opponents with a Koosh ball and send him (or her) into "jail," off to the sidelines. You can't cross the mid-line, or you're jailed too.

3 If you end up in jail, form a line with the rest of your inmates.

4 If one of your throws is caught, not only do you have to go to jail, but whoever is standing at the head of the line in your opponents' jail gets back in the game. A double whammy.

5 Your team wins when all your opponents are in jail.

Spud

This is a classic. You'll need at least 3 or 4 players, although any number can play.

1 One person holds the Koosh ball. They will start the round. Everyone else gathers around and waits expectantly.

2 As soon as he feels ready, the person holding the ball throws it high into the air straight up and simultaneously shouts one of the other player's names. He (or she) is the "Spud."

3 Everybody else scatters. The Spud has to try to catch the throw. As soon as he gets control of it, he shouts "Spud!" and all the other players have to freeze.

4 The Spud then takes 4 giant steps toward the nearest potential victim and tries to hit him with a well-placed throw. The victim is not allowed to dodge and can only move in an effort to catch the ball.

5 If the thrower connects, the victim picks up the letter "S." If the throw is caught, or if it misses completely, it goes the other way—the thrower picks up the letter. For the next go round, the "Spud" is the player who picked up the last letter, and he or she starts the next round.

6 If you pick up all four letters, "S P U D", you have to bow out. Last one in the game is the winner.

Electric Koosh

A great party game. Requires at least 9 people, but more makes it better. Hundreds would be ideal.

1 Everyone has to sit down in two parallel teams, face to face, a few feet apart. The same number of people in each line. Set the Koosh ball on the ground at the end of the lines, exactly in the middle between the last two people and an arm's length from both.

2 Somebody has to be the referee. He (or she) sits at the head of the two lines with a coin.

3 Now for the icky part. Everybody has to hold hands with the person next to them. Not only that, but everybody (except for the two people at the head of their line) has to close their eyes.

14

4 The two people at the head of the lines are the watchers. No one is allowed to say a word. The referee flips the coin, covers it, then uncovers it.

5 If it's tails, nobody does anything except get nervous. If it's heads, it's a hand-squeezing electricity race, starting with the watcher who squeezes his neighbor's hand, who squeezes her neighbor's hand, who squeezes his neighbor's hand...

6 The last person in the line sits, poised. When he or she feels the squeeze, they grab the Koosh ball as fast as possible. The winning line gets to shift. The last person goes to the head of the line and everybody scoots down one. When the first person gets back to the head, that line is declared the official Electric Koosh winner.

7 One last point. If a false alarm is sounded—if your watcher mistakenly sends a squeeze down the line when the coin wasn't heads—then the line has to shift *back* one spot.

KooshWear

Koosh balls make highly unusual fashion statements. If you didn't cut off the loops that your Koosh ball came equipped with, here are a couple of your options:

- A HUGE rubber ring that you can also use as a yo-yo.
- A really squeezable bunny tail.
- A shoe pom-pom that gets noticed.
- A key chain you can hang from your pocket (and just *try* to lose it in your purse).
- History's largest rubberized ponytail pom-pom.
- A sock pom-pom that will put all the others to shame.

Table Koosh

This is a cafeteria game, playable right up to when the bell rings. For two players.

1 Players sit down at opposite ends of the table. Clear off any debris in the way.

2 The object is to toss the Koosh ball in such a way that it lands within a hand's span of the other guy's edge. If it does, the tosser scores 3 points. If it actually lands *on* the edge, overhanging it, that's a touchdown—6 points. If it goes over the edge, that's minus one point.

3 Whoever has the most points when the bell rings is the winner.

OVER HANGING EDGE

Hall Koosh

A specialized college game, extremely useful in dormitories where the hallways and evenings are often long and frequently a little dreary.

1 You'll need a long hallway as a playing field. For teams, 1 or 2 players each should do it.

2 Set up in the middle of the hallway. Each team is defending its end of the hallway. Decide which team

18

starts. They get the Koosh ball and attempt to throw it by the other team, which attempts to block or intercept the throw.

3 You can't advance the ball by running with it, you have to throw it by the defender(s). Once it's been thrown, it's up for grabs. Anyone can get it. No physical interference is allowed, although you can stand directly in front of someone trying to throw, then holler, jump up and down and otherwise be intimidating.

4 A point is scored by hitting the end of the hallway, after which a new round is started.

Stand-Off

This is a relative of "Guts," a competitive Frisbee game that demands a steely gaze, a strong throwing arm and asbestos catching hands. With the Koosh ball, there's no need for the asbestos.

1 Stand-Off can be played between teams or individuals, it doesn't matter.

2 Separate the players by at least 10 good strides, but play this by ear. It depends more than anything on the kinds of throwing arms you're dealing with.

20

3 The object is to throw the Koosh ball by the other player(s). The throws can be as hard as you like, but they have to be within reach of the receiver. Any throw out of this strike zone is counted as a point for the receiver(s).

4 If no one touches the ball—and it *was* touchable— 1 point for the thrower. If it's knocked down—no points for anyone. If it's caught—1 point for the catcher.

5 Alternate throws. The winner is the first one to 21 points.

Volley

This is the basic 2-person game of Koosh ball. It's a free-form game that can be played on any level from family-hour cooperative to bloodthirsty competitive.

1 Using your hands, begin volleying the Koosh ball back and forth. No catching and no throwing.

2 Back up as the two of you get a little better. You don't need much space and in fact Volley is a good indoor game if you can keep away from the Ming vases and the rest of the breakables.

3 To play cooperatively, all you need to do is count consecutive hits. To play competitively, draw court boundaries and try to put the Koosh ball on the ground in the other player's court. Incidentally, for an advanced version of the game, use your feet and knees.

Racket Catch

A two-person game of "Koosh tennis." All you'll need is a pair of tennis rackets. The kind that you'll find buried in the closet should work fine.

1 Distribute the two rackets evenly among players.

2 The object is to both catch and toss the Koosh ball with the rackets. When you're catching, you have to wield the racket gently so that the ball will stay on it. With a little practice, you ought to be able to sling and catch a Koosh ball clear across the yard.

3 You can play Racket Catch competitively simply by setting consecutive catch records. (Incidentally, if you'd like a slower version of plain tennis, a Koosh ball is plenty sturdy enough to take the abuse. Just forget about the bounces.)

Koosh Golf

This is one of those games where everybody really has to have a Koosh ball. Besides that, all you'll need is unsupervised access to a few pots and pans in the kitchen, and some open space to work with.

1 Collect a half-dozen or so pots and pans and place them strategically around your yard. This is a critical part of the game, so don't neglect it. Put the pans behind things like dog houses, way up on top of things (in the fork of a tree?) Put them near hazards (a sleeping grown-up?), or float them in a pool if you're so lucky.

2 After you ve designed your course, as imaginatively as possible, gather all your golfers together at the starting line, at least 30 or 40 steps away from your first pan ("hole").

3 Everybody takes turns trying to land their Koosh ball in each of the pans. Any misses have to be picked up, and, without changing position, thrown again from that point. Count throws. Winner has the fewest throws after going through the entire course.

TowelCatch

You'll need a bath towel for every player. This is one of those "no-hands" games that takes a little bit of practice.

1 The object of the game is to pass and catch the Koosh back and forth using just the towels. This takes a little getting used to, particularly when any accuracy is called for.

2 The technique is to hold the towel loosely between two hands at about waist height. Put the Koosh ball in the middle of the towel and snap it taut. The resulting trampoline action will shoot the Koosh out, and a little practice will help direct it. If you use a big bath towel and roll up the ends so you'll have something to grab on to, you'll have a good bit more success.

3 Catching is done by relaxing the towel and catching it in the middle.

4 You can play the game cooperatively just by setting consecutive catch records. Note: Experienced towel snappers are able to play this game across a 20 or 30 yard playing field.

Koosh Paddle

To play Koosh Paddle, you really need to run out and get one of those little wooden paddles that comes with a rubber ball on an elastic band.

1 Pull off the elastic band and ball. Those things are too hard to hit anyway.

2 Find yourself a partner similarly equipped and spread yourselves out. Fifteen or twenty feet to start with.

3 Begin batting the Koosh ball back and forth. You can warm up by setting consecutive records.

4 The competitive version is modeled after badminton; only the net is imaginary. You can play doubles or singles. Both teams settle on out-of-bound lines and agree to the height of the "net." Serving is alternated every five serves and the object of the game is to put the ball on the ground in the other player's court. Only one hit per side and twenty-one points wins.

Kooshoes

A 2-person Kooshy version of horseshoes.

1 Collect a couple of deep pans from the kitchen and march outside with them.

2 Separate the pans by 15 medium paces and draw a 2-foot circle around each of them.

3 Station your partner behind one of the pans and yourself behind the other. Alternate turns and try to drop perfect tosses into the pans for 3 points. Leaning a Koosh ball up against the pan will get you 2 points. Just landing within the "close-enough" circle scores a single point.

4 First one to 11 is the winner.

Juggling

J uggling is a bit of age-old anti-gravity magic that can turn anybody's stagnant career or social life right around. Unfortunately, a lot of people, particularly those who could most benefit, have been put off by the apparent difficulties. For these people—the klutz majority—the Koosh balls are the answer to their collective prayer. They're easy to catch, they don't bounce around, roll away or make a mess on the floor.

1 Juggling is the art of great throws, not great catches. Practice with only one Koosh ball. Toss it back and forth from one hand to the other. About as high as your eyes, and as wide as your body. Try to land the ball directly in the middle of your waiting hand. This is target practice, not catching practice.

2 This is the big step. It may take 20 minutes, it may take 2 days, but anybody who can scratch their nose in the dark can learn it.

Hold both Koosh balls, one in each hand. Do not be afraid. Think for a second. You are going to toss one ball up into the air. It will pass in front of your eyes on its way to your other hand. But your other hand is already occupied. This is a problem. You can solve this problem by any of three ways: First, you can panic and just fling the other ball out of the way. Second, you can cheat and pass the ball being held to your other, recently vacated, hand. Then you'll catch the flying Koosh ball and think you've done something clever.

Or third, you can choose the true way, the only way, the Righteous Path.

PANIC STEP 1.

PANIC STEP 2.

CHEAT STEP 1.

CHEAT STEP 2.

CHEAT STEP 3.

As the flying Koosh ball peaks in front of your eyes, do not panic, do not cheat. Wait until this very moment to toss the second ball just to the inside of the dropping ball on an identical—reverse direction—arc. It should go back to your other hand where you will probably have to make a desperate lunge to try to catch it.

Both Koosh balls are tossed up, one after another on identical arcs that cross directly over the hand that makes the second toss. Don't forget to practice going both ways. Start with your right hand, do that for a while, then start with your left. Confused? Look at the illustrations.

RIGHT TO LEFT

34

RIGHTEOUS PATH

LEFT TO RIGHT

Going on to 3 Koosh balls is no big deal IF you've spent enough time with two. If you haven't, this part could be exciting. You're ready for 3 when you can toss 2 back and forth without cheating, without panicking, and without having to dive for the second catch.

If you're ready, great. Here we go.

3 Put 2 Koosh balls in one hand, one in the other. Relax. You'll start tossing from the hand with two. A ball will go up, pass in front of your eyes and begin dropping into your other occupied hand. No need to panic. Just toss the second ball up exactly as you're supposed to have been practicing. Nothing new here. The only new part comes now.

STEP 1.   (OLD STUFF)

STEP 2.   (OLD STUFF)

STEP 3.   (OLD STUFF)

STEP 4.   (NEW STUFF)

STEP 5.   (NEW STUFF)

STEP 6.   THE END

As this second toss goes through the top of *its* arc, now you have to toss the third ball just to the inside of it as it drops down into your hand.

Count as you go through this bit of excitement: One toss … two toss … three toss.

If you can do this much, take a bow. That's a jug, the unit of juggling. All that stands between you and a long rewarding career in the circus is practice. Once you can do three tosses without lunging all over the room, try four … five … six … etc. The moves are identical. As each Koosh ball drops in, toss the ball in the waiting hand right by it.

Incidentally, for more information and a fuller description, try the book *Juggling for the Complete Klutz*, available at any self-respecting bookstore.

37

Footbag Koosh

Footbag is an ancient Asian street game recently popularized in the U.S. At its simplest, it's nothing but a game of catch—with one change: players use their feet instead of their hands. The Koosh ball is a great footbag substitute because of the fact that it is soft, doesn't bounce strangely, and won't roll under the furniture.

At first, "foot catch" like this appears flat-out impossible. But feet are capable of a lot more than we normally ask of them. A few hours of practice can give you some amazing moves. Here are some tips:

1 Begin by tossing (with your hand) the Koosh ball up and directly in front of you, so that it lands about a step away. Before it hits the ground though, step forward and bring your foot directly up under it. Use the side of your foot and don't think of "kicking" the ball, think of "boosting" it from underneath. Done correctly, the ball will then pop up in front of your eyes.

2 Practice by yourself with both feet. After you find a partner, toss back and forth with well placed little tosses. The idea is to boost the Koosh ball accurately enough so that you can bump it back, foot-to-foot.

3 There are actually 5 different kicks. The illustrations should help you get the idea for each, but the tricks for every one of them are the same:

- wait until the Koosh ball is near the ground before contacting it

- really concentrate on the Koosh ball so that you can connect squarely with it

KNEE KICK

- turn your foot so that the side (flat) part of your foot makes the connection

- practice with a partner and remember, this is a tricky game that takes practice, but once you start to get it, it's a whole lot of fun.

TOE KICK

BACK KICK

OUTSIDE KICK

Koosh Tag

A slight variation on an old favorite.

1 Whoever's "it" has the Koosh ball. Everyone else has to run around like mad so they can't be hit by the Koosh thrower. If they are, then they're "it."

2 You can make the game a little harder by requiring everyone to throw with their "wrong" hand, or by specifying only certain body parts as being eligible targets.

Circle Chase

Another party game requiring a good number of players, at least 8 or 9.

1 Everybody sits down in a circle facing in. One player gets up, takes the Koosh ball and begins walking around the circle very ominously.

2 Suddenly, for no apparent reason, the walker drops the ball onto the head of the one of the sitters, and simultaneously takes off running around the outside of the circle.

3 Whoever got Kooshed then has to grab the ball, get up and give chase in the same direction. If they aren't able to bounce the ball off the runner's back before he (or she) can get around the circle 3 times and back to their vacated spot, then the chaser becomes the Koosh ball dropper, and it starts all over. Otherwise, the chaser tries again.

No-Hands Koosh

Catching Koosh balls is a whole lot more challenging if you make one simple change: no hands. Here's how the game is played.

1 Back away from your partner as many feet as you think the two of you can manage, then toss him (or her) the Koosh ball. They will then have one

panic-stricken second to twist themselves into some kind of shape to make
a no-hands catch. Some suggestions:
teeth, knees, shoulders, heads, back
of the neck . . . All you need is a little
physical imagination and loose joints.

2 The cooperative
way to play the
game is to tally up
consecutive catches,
and set your own
records.

3 Or, if you're a little bloodthirstier
than that, you can play a competitive
version of the game: toss the Koosh ball
in an easy arc (no fair pelting your
opponent) and then hope that he (or she)
muffs it. If they do, score one for your side.
After that, it's your turn. First one to 10
catches is the winner.

Koosh Attack

This is a field game where everybody has to have one Koosh ball. It's a free-form game of tag, played (hopefully) in a big open space.

46

1 Gather as many Koosh-equipped players together as possible. Then everybody should troop on out to a big open playing area.

2 Divide into two teams and pick two jails at opposite ends of the field. Trees make pretty good jails.

3 Both teams gather together near their jails for a pep rally, and, at a signal, start the game. The object is to "capture" as many of your opponents as possible by bouncing a Koosh ball off them. When they're captured, they have to go to the enemy home base. As long as they're captured, they have to keep a hand on the base, or at least a hand on somebody else who's got a hand on it.

4 Captives can be freed only by a tag from one of their uncaptured teammates. And they cannot be freed while "in transit" after being captured. They have to be at the enemy home base.

5 Nobody can carry more than one Koosh ball although it doesn't have to be the one they started with. And there is no "home base" where you can't be captured. It's a total free-for-all.

6 First team to capture all its opponents is the winner.

Koosh Squoosh

A cooperative, no-scoring kind of game. Best played with friends or a group that's interested in getting that way.

1 First off, everybody gets in a line. The idea is to pass the Koosh ball from person to person down the line, without the use of any hands. This takes relaxed inhibitions and physical imagination. An old party favorite is to carry it between your chin and chest, but you can easily improve on that. Try trapping it between your knees, balancing it on your shoulder, trapping it against your side, squooshing it between your toes...

Cut n' Run Koosh

This is a Koosh ball variation on backyard football. It's usually played with 3 or 4, but a few more are ok.

1 The idea is to complete passes and move the ball downfield. The quarterback is not allowed to run.

50

2 You'll need a quarterback and one defender per receiver. Quarterback and receiver huddle up and draw a pass pattern in the dirt. The only limitation: the receiver can make only 2 cuts. You can't run around like crazy until you're open.

3 On a signal, the receiver snaps the Koosh ball back to the quarterback and starts his pattern. Running in a straight line is fine, but two cuts are all you get.

4 No pass rush allowed. Three incomplete passes or one interception and the quarterback, receiver and defender all change places.

Koosh Pickle

A classic baseball game that can be improved with the addition of the Koosh ball and one new rule.

1 Three players, two bases, and one Koosh ball make for all your equipment needs.

2 One player is the runner, the other two are the basemen and toss the ball back and forth. Whenever the runner feels so bold, he (or she) can venture out between the bases. His (or her) object is to get to the other base safely, without being tagged out.

3 If the runner is tagged, whoever makes the tag becomes the runner. So far, this is just like the hardball version of pickle, but you can add another rule with the no-bruise Koosh ball.

4 In Koosh Pickle, the runner is allowed to knock the ball down, or otherwise get in its way, so as to keep the baseman from catching it.

Hopskoosh

opskoosh is played, not too surprisingly, on a hopscotch court. The object of the game is to own as many of the squares as possible. The rules go like this:

1 Draw a hopscotch court with chalk and put your Koosh ball in the number one square. Any square occupied by the ball is off-limits. Nobody can land on it.

2 Start from behind the court and hop, one footed, into the number two square. Then, one-footed again, into the number three square. Then jump and straddle-land with one foot in four and one foot in five.

3 Hop one-footed into six, and then straddle-land on seven and eight.

4 Jump straight into the air, turn around and come back down facing the opposite direction, with one foot in seven and one foot in eight.

5 Now go back down the court the same way, hopping and straddling. When you get to one and two, you can't put a foot into one (since it's occupied by the Koosh ball) so land with one foot on two and, while balancing there, reach over and pick up the ball.

6 Turn around and toss the Koosh ball onto an unoccupied square. That becomes your square. Put your name on it, then hand the Koosh ball over to the next player.

7 The next player then puts the Koosh ball in square number one and starts the same routine with one difference: he can't land in your square, he has to skip it.

8 Anyone who lands on a line, or falls over into a heap, loses their turn. The winner is the one with the most squares when the game ends.

Bop the Brother

You don't really have to have a brother for this one, sisters will do fine, as well as neighbors, friends, parents, relatives...

This is a great indoor game if you can find a room without breakables. It has been extensively house-tested, and it *does* break the lamps (but we still play it).

1 Best played with just 2 or 3. Everyone can have a Koosh ball, or you can make do with just one. You'll also need a stuffed chair or sofa for every player.

2 The chairs and sofas should be pretty close to one another to make it interesting. Everybody hunkers down behind their chair and proceeds to lob throws over the other guy's chair.

3 If you get bopped, you have to report it. That counts as a point for the other guy. Since this is an indoor game, and since everybody should be down below their furniture forts, only lobbing is permitted—no speed balling. That's the outside version (known as "Warm Weather Snowball Fighting").

4 The game ends when somebody gets a million points.

Off the Wall

An outdoor game that can also be played indoors with understanding grown-ups. You'll need a wall that you can safely pelt (no windows).

1 Somebody (let's say you) starts. You're the thrower. The catcher puts his (or her) back to you and faces the wall, about an arm's length away from it.

2 With absolutely no warning, haul off and throw the Koosh ball against the wall, above your catcher's head. The idea is to throw it so hard—or so soft—that your catcher won't be able to grab it before it hits the ground. (The best strategy is to alternate fastballs with lobbers randomly).

3 You can throw it as high as you like (without hitting the ceiling if you're indoors) but you can't throw it lower than head height. If you throw it too low, or off to one side more than an arm's length, you lose the point. If you bean your catcher, you lose the point and have to apologize nicely. If you're having arguments, draw lines on the ground to indicate arm's width. (Hint: When you're catching, listen for the incoming "whoosh" for some idea of what kind of throw is coming.)

4 Everybody takes turns throwing and catching. First one to catch 10 is the winner. Or, you can work as a team and set consecutive catch records.

Customized Koosh Balls

Bolo Koosh

All you'll need is two Koosh balls and a good quality rubber band or three. By using the loops (which you weren't supposed to have cut off) on the Koosh balls, you can connect two of them with rubber bands. With a bolo, you can definitely make Koosh games a lot trickier. Try just plain catch for starters.

60

Indoor Fuzzy Dice

You'll need a bunch of rubber bands for this one. Link them all together into one long rubber band, and then link the Koosh ball onto the end of it. String two of these up from the ceiling somewhere and it makes the world's first pair of indoor fuzzy dice. Impossible to leave alone.

Darts-on-a-Leash

If you only have one Koosh ball, you can play a version of darts-on-a-leash. String your tether up close enough to a wall so that you can stretch the Koosh ball back, release it, and whap the wall. Now set up a dart board-sized target on the wall and score a point for every bull's eye.

Beach Koosh

The Koosh ball, bless its buoyant little rubber soul, floats in salt water. Try the following game the next time you're at the beach.

1 Someone has to stay on the beach, everyone else in the water, waist deep or a little deeper.

2 The thrower is on the beach. The catchers are in the water. The thrower has to lob sky balls—as high as possible—to his catchers. The catchers have to circle underneath and compete for the catch. Getting position is obviously critical and most anything is legal during this phase.

3 Whoever makes the catch returns the Koosh ball to the thrower and it starts over. When one catcher has three catches to his credit, he or she switches with the thrower.

Pool Koosh

Koosh balls will float in salt water and sink slowly in fresh water, which makes the following game possible. You'll need a pool, at least two players, one Koosh ball, and a hot day.

1 Pick two teams (even if they're only one person each). Everybody lines up on the edge of the pool, their backs to the water. Somebody tosses the Koosh ball over their head into the pool. At the sound of the splash, everybody turns around, jumps in and tries to get it first.

64

2 The team with the ball then tries to swim it to "their" side of the pool. If they're tagged before they get there, they have to toss the ball back into the middle of the pool. Passing is allowed, as is splashing and all sorts of distracting noises. Dropped Koosh balls, or intercepted passes, go over to the other side.

Nose Bonk

Because of the Koosh ball's essentially kind-hearted nature, you can fearlessly play a few games of catch that would threaten a good beak-squashing with something like a baseball.

1 Playable with any number from two up, indoors or out.

2 Everybody lays down head to head and starts tossing and catching the Koosh ball back and forth in high arcs that would terminate on somebody's nose. The object is to make the nose-saving catch, toss the ball back, and do it all without laughing. It's not easy.

3 Spread out the better you get. Try setting consecutive catch records or, for serious players, change the rules like this: If a toss is so perfect that it will land *directly* on your nose, you have to let it go. Then everyone gets to yell: "NOSE BONK!"

Kooshy Kooshy Koo

You haven't lived until you've scrubbed with a Koosh ball.

Mail Order Information

Other Books Available from Klutz Press:

The Aerobie Book

The Unbelievable Bubble Book

The Klutz Book of Card Games:
For Sharks and Others

KidsGardening: A Kid's Guide to Messing Around
in the Dirt

Country and Blues Guitar for the Musically Hopeless

Country and Blues Harmonica for the
Musically Hopeless

The Hacky Sack Book

The Klutz Book of Jacks

The Klutz Book of Marbles

Juggling for the Complete Klutz

KidsCooking: A Very Slightly Messy Manual

Kidsongs

Kidsongs 2

The Klutz Book of Knots

The Official Koosh Book

The Klutz Book of Magic

The World's Tackiest Postcards

Revenge of the Son of the World's Tackiest Postcards

Pumping Plastic: A 6-Week Jump Rope Workout

The Klutz Yo-Yo Book

Koosh Balls $4.95 each

For people interested in starting a galloping herd of multi-colored Koosh balls, here's your chance.

Mondo Koosh Balls
$9.95 each

Just off the production line! Koosh balls on steroids. Bigger, bulkier, more cuddly than ever. About the size of a softball, these are Koosh balls for people with bigger Koosh ball needs.

See ordering information on next page.

MAIL ORDER BLANK

Quantity	Description	Price
	Add $3.00 for Postage	
	Total Enclosed (check or money order)	

Name _____

Street _____

Address _____

KO Klutz Enterprises / 2121 Staunton Ct. / Palo Alto CA 94306

Order Koosh balls ($4.95 each), Mondo koosh balls ($9.95 each), and additional copies of *The Official Koosh Book* ($9.95, complete with Koosh ball) through the mail. Add $3.00 for shipping. Please use the order form above and note that prices are guaranteed only through 1990. Afterwards, call or write for a current catalogue. If you would like a FREE catalogue, use an order form on the next page.

- -

KO

FREE CATALOGUE FORM

The *FLYING APPARATUS CATALOGUE* is filled with unicycles, jugggling paraphernalia, kites and who knows what all. It's available free for the asking. Call us at (415) 424-0739, or write.

Name _____

Street _____

Town/State _____

Zip _____

Klutz Press   2121 Staunton Ct.   Palo Alto, CA 94306